Down

by

the

Riverside

Ways

Also by Susan Allison

The Ibis in the Buttonwood Tree (1999)

Down by the Riverside Ways

Poems

Susan Allison

The Buttonwood Tree
Middletown, CT

Antrim House

Simsbury, Connecticut

Library of Congress Control Number: 2009922377

ISBN 978-0-9817883-3-3

Printed & bound by United Graphics, Inc.

First Edition, 2009

Book design: Rennie McQuilkin
Photograph of author: Rennie McQuilkin
Bridge photographs: Susan Allison

Antrim House
860.217.0023
AntrimHouse@comcast.net
www.AntrimHouseBooks.com
P.O. Box 111, Tariffville, CT 06081

Acknowledgments

Thanks to the editors of the following journals, where poems from this collection first appeared:

Ferment Press: "The Day the Poets Came to Town"

Ugly Duckling Press: "Meditation"

Thanks also to the Middletown Commission on the Arts, which underwrote publication of *The Ibis in the Buttonwood Tree.*

And very special thanks to those who have supported me in many ways over the years: Mom, Dad, Cindy, Richard, Stephan and John, Tony Connor, Betsy Morgan, Kathleen White, John Basinger, Kate Rushin, Sarah McQuilkin, Rennie McQuilkin, Sharon Charde, and Abigail Reynolds.

To Stephan and John

for love supreme, humor, dishes, and stories

Table of Contents

I. Prelude

II. The Good Life

III. Sidewalk Legends

No one can advise or help you — no one.

from LETTERS TO A YOUNG POET, Rainer Maria Rilke

Prelude

I have written your names on my cheekbone.

from "Call," Audre Lorde

Mockingbird

I sing for unknown reasons,
not like Whitman, proud peacock,
or Maya, genius bird.
I sing prompted, tense of tongue,
recalcitrant, fatigued, yet
seized by notions of flagrant life
and warnings from Rilke and Lorde
that silence in such circumstance
is tantamount to dying.

Pale mother of aging social grace
who may never know,
though I warble in imitation of
birds of brighter color,
the creation springs of choir song
in whose essential splendor
comes news of earth itself,
I sing urgent strains of coming change
In every copied hymn.

As widows in their beds undressed
from day's impostured roles
read of lives in different skins yet
putting down their books behold
their own hands frame the page
and back to life are sentenced,
so memory and household words

define daily
what can and cannot be.

What is mine to other lives?
What are the psalms we are singing?
The few awake can hear the song.
A nightingale? No, only
the mockingbird repeating
refrains of missive phrases
like half remembered folk songs
as faces blend with faces
and claim joyous night through dreaming.

Like a mockingbird I sing alone—
melodies, rhythms, words
burn in my heart through other birds
whose messages astound,
whose brilliant lives aloof from mine
renew the world through sound.
I understudy twilight song,
in hours between meanings,
uncaged, unproud, and singing.

The Good Life

*Sometimes we touch a body and we wake it and
it is a way through the night which opens to our
senses the pulsing of its arms like the sea's.*

from EYES TO SEE OTHERWISE, Homero Aridjis
(translated by W.S. Merwin)

Ibis Lost

I snuck out at night toward the Sound—
into my parents' back yard,
across the wet grass to the East River,
through the crackly salt marsh,
mud and crabs, humid sulfur air.
I was often out past dawn when first
sunlight hits the rising river mist
in traveling bands of rainbows and gold.

Too old to be living with my parents.
Too young to understand anything.
Just right to be behaving as I was.
I danced to the river all alone
like some crazed giant bird.
I moved my back and my shoulders
in and out, and I knew,
I could feel.

Sunset

Sitting late day on my front porch,
the scorned neighborhood hippy,
I saw that young girl
who was always alone,
roller skating up Cascade Hill.
She wore a magenta coat, a gold yellow cap,
and oversized, turquoise pants.
Her arms swinging, pumping,
strenuous right foot left foot right foot left foot...
Then, just past the hill's crest
she rolled, gliding down like a champion falcon,
arms outstretched.
She was the sunset.
She was my whole damn day.

The Good Life

The thing about good living
is that it happens, despite
plotting and planning, it happens
contrary to all devices. It happens
when you are renting the only room
you can afford and you somehow
catch the way the light is coming through
the broken dirty windows.
The door is open
and the wind blows in like balm.
It's warm and you see the colors of the
faded gray frame of the door
against the rust-colored leaves
in the small patch of jungle
down by the alley.
The good life
comes through your eyes
and your ears and your skin
the way a wild animal comes at you
when it is just curious.

Kitchen Home

A simple basket
with vegetables
and fruits on the table
as in gardens.
I learn to love
standing near the stove
stirring soup
or watching jasmine
flowers dance
in a boil.
The eyes of cats peer
with simmering purrs
from bowls of ivy;
the scent of grapefruit
peels and ginseng linger
until late morning.
On coldest days
I dream in brewing pots
and toast my loaves
golden brown.
I pray in orange ginger.

The Void I Am Not

No occasion
no obligatory vacation
no relatives
no schedules
just breathing
as if
breath
is everything
molecular tides
bird song
everything
in tune—
the social grace
of sun
to moon.

Meditation

Every night as the sun draws in his hot breath
and holds it,
waiting for the moon to arch her back
across the sky,
I move in the same design as the others.

We sing together hymns of suffering
and liberation,
though we've never seen one another.
The pleasure is sensuous, like remedy, like
excitation,

when we meet in corresponding nature
and we know each other only in these times
of inmost clarity
when we move together.

A Tune for Harmonica

for Thomas Moses

Ladder ladder I descend
down where cocktail parties end.
Landscaped vistas, rarified air—
it's too freezing cold up there.
Moribund hostesses make me shiver.
I am climbing a ladder down to the river.

Rippled current ocean-bound,
only here do I bow down,
sink my toes in fish-rank muck
soft and warm and full of suck.
My harp sings to the blessing giver.
I am climbing her ladder down by the river.

Thanks

His comforting
is like ice on a cold day.
Be that as it may,
I love this man
in clever ways.
And he don't care
where I go
as long as
I come back.
Even now,
as strange stories erupt,
we gossip together
on the porch steps.

Greensleeves

Stephan is a cold tree in winter
unyielding, unbending, hard
limbs outstretched with frozen sap
stiff in the frigid wind
for green leaves to dance in the spring.

Wife Reading

Once someone said
"You read too much into things."

I read the moon
rolling around our bedroom floor,
Saile's toy moon-ball
sneaking into our room—Saile
is awake, we are not,
we want to sleep. He
follows the moon.
I read the mattress after you are
out of bed. Your dreams, sexual as usual,
feel weightless, fragrant.
I am a marigold
as it rests against the purring body
of a cat
sleeping in the sun.
I read Saile's face: full.
He will surely take me where
he wants to go today.
I have read the stars, the traffic
and random motions.
I approach you, always reading.
It is the windiest, sunniest,
starkest, most impassioned of days.
The wind, the trees are crying out:
Get real sister!

I have read your love
kissing by the river,
secretly rocking my bones.
I read the spring
and hope that by gazing
in my rapture, I will align,
inspired.
It is spring
and world-joy bursts
from every bloom,
phoebes in the woodbine singing.
I read the light this morning,
the light you bring into the house
first thing
every morning, creaking
across the wooden floors,
cracking the windows for light
and air and noise.
At the end of the day
I read the lines on your face,
how you try, how your love
weighs you down. You move
slowly, deliberately, and
carry Saile up to bed.
The years settle with persistence.
As I stand and look out the screen door

I read the moon as it rolls around the sky:
love remains gentle,
vast in rhythm, light of God.
My body warms
from the depths of the world
into prayer.

Cub

Nature mom and cub
swinging in the trees.
He is naked, nursing
in a new hammock.
I too am shirtless now.

Cub watches the green leaves
as he rests in my arms.
He is wood spirit like his father.
I sing to him of the green leaves,
then he pees, poops, pukes
all over me, and then he smiles.

Young cub, I profess
my love for you.
There is no more joy
in all the world
than in your eyes.

Life and death were never
until you made them whole.

The Myth of Sisyphus

for Butch Peña

I am fighting again,
trying to keep myself
together, pushing myself.
And in my kitchen frenzy
I blurt to my husband
my bleak outlook.
He prospects:
"Think of Sisyphus"
which only enrages me
further: "Is that the best
you can come up with!"
I should take comfort
in knowing my life is somehow
better than the classic
archetype of futility.
I slam the cupboard door
on our collection of
donated canned foods,
endeavoring to create
a lunch to send to school
with Saile. I pick through
the nuts left over from
Thanksgiving, crack them
to amass a small pile, soak
the carrots in water
to revive some crunch.

That night it snows.
Next morning
Saile leaps
into our morning bed,
flings curtains wide.
Impatient for the slopes,
he hops about our
immobile limbs.
When we get to Foss Hill
I watch him
endlessly slide down
run up
slide down
as if each time
is the first. Finally
I get it.
Saile offers me the sled.
I freefall with abandon
down the snowy hill.
I am no longer Sisyphus,
I am the boulder.

Reunion with Kella

We talked in foreign languages,
a mouthwash of speeches.
Your parents, my parents
new in the new neighborhood,
in from Bogotá and Connecticut,
landing on 3600 and 3602
Fallen Timber Drive,
neighbors on a road paved
through fallen timber
for a suburb in Kentucky.
Twenty years later and it's
–Shit Suzie, you sound like a hick.
–Well you started it.
–Who the hell we bein' now?
Remember the time
we drove back home
passing cows and more cows
and we slept in the red bunk beds
where your brothers used to sleep?
We got junk drunk that night
and played pool
with the cute pool shark
and his motorcycle buddies.
You got so rude
to the ex-marine,
admonishing him like a school boy.
I felt so proud of you,

my bombshell friend.
We hung out that night
in parking lots and pool halls.
It was like old times in the back room
of the liquor store stocked with
BUD wahyzur and MAR bros.
We laughed so hard
we could hardly talk at all,
like our old convulsions
in church pews and station wagons.
We let the nice guys drive us home
and made it back to the red bunk beds.
We stayed up all night and we couldn't
figure out our accents,
you part Bowling Green,
part Boston slang, and me
with this distasteful Connecticut Snobie,
now home in the place where we once
collected accents like crazy,
trying them on like shoes and
wearing them especially if they didn't fit.
We spole like Greta Garbo ("Daarling,
I am afraaa'd of no-thing but bore-dom")
or our own version of Chinese
that sounded more like Russian
("CHEE yong Drivink?").
Our favorite was British Royalty.

We din wanna talk like our NAYburs
but we usually did.
Wango swimmin?
What ever happened to those NAYburs?
Pappy, the JARboes, and those
ubiquitous spinster sisters?
Where did they go?
And their yard full of painted
white rocks—where did it go?
–Girl, our accents are out there.
–Talkin everything at once.
–Like hair in the wind.
I asked "Did you get his ad-DRESS?" and
you said
"Honey, ya cain't screw an ADD-ress."

Broomstick

C'mon broomstick, let's fly.
Rise above these rooftops
and soar like demon angels
to the moon.
C'mon broomstick,
dust your rickety self off
and we'll transform this lonely night
into the holy fury of love's survival.
And we'll sweep like nothing
has swept before,
sweep the pale stars
right off the evening's shoulder,
roll into midnight
swift as falcons fly,
draw the moon down into
our breasts and greet
the wind as we turn
miracles out of our own
darkness, unashamed.
C'mon broomstick honey,
trust me.

My God's Desire

Evening in an amber light far
from the bright rooms of boisterous,
drinking, blessèd friends celebrating,
I submit to a desirous and de-limbed god
returning and eager to be reconnected,
back from the voyage, un-beleaguered.
I speak oracles to him and he ravishes me well.
I roll in his storm-rocked waves,
compelled to find him, unite him,
arouse life and bring death.
And in grateful paradise we resurrect
ourselves and come back breath by breath.

Slipknot for a Hurricane

You sleep on the boat
with my long black shirt
wrapped around your neck
like a scarf. Hot sun
makes my shirt smell like me
and you smell like you.
Perfume. Heat. Our smells together
rise from your body.
I am nearby rowing
in a small boat
approaching
like that lone duck we saw
waiting
for the right time
to snatch the bread
we'd tossed.
You look like a woman
from a distance.
Soft tanned body
curves down
like smoke.
Genie body.
Ancient man.
Gentle currents.
I row closer
slowly now

dipping my oars into the river.
I tie my line to yours
the way you taught me.
A slipknot
but strong enough
for a hurricane.

I Heard the Angel Singing

So so so so sometimes
there co co coco comes
so soso so so some lo lo lo
lo love that's no
no no no no popo po
po po po poetry's business.

Sidewalk Legends

O body swayed to music,
O brightening glance,
How can we know the dancer
From the dance?

from "Among School Children,"
William Butler Yeats

Choose Any River

Choose any river
north south east west
Tigris Columbia Amazon Nile
Po Mississippi Quinetucket,
the Long Tidal River.
Our people, you and I,
north south east west
have always grown beside it
as now here in Middletown,
on this long river, at this bend,
under this bridge.

The early English
pushed the Wangunks
across the river to the east
and there are traces of migrations:
Japanese Dragons
who left footprints in the clay.
Our land broke from Morocco
before glaciers slept like giants
that thawed into a deluge
leaving crack and crevice fashioned
into channels of expansion
north south east west
and this river rose and fell,
slid across alluvial plains,
making networks out of fissures,

marking history with its flow
as if God had cast a spell
making heaven out of hell for
canoes, boats, ferries, bridges.

Choose any bend, you'll find a bridge
for people, coaches, trains and cars.
North south east west
the river passes pastures, rills and farms,
rolling verdant hillsides,
sheep and cows and horses.
Then come around the great bend…

It is the Seventeenth Century—
a fledgling harbor grows.
There's a meeting house near
a large elm tree, now dead
in Riverside Cemetery...

It is the Eighteenth Century—
silver, men and industry
feed the Revolution
and the bustling harbor rivals
Boston or New York in size,
in wealth, in ships, supplies
of spice and slaves, tobacco, rum,
sugar, tea, and opium...

It is the Nineteenth Century—
manufacture creates

guns and more for civil war.
And rifts in the commonwealth
create the common poor.
Manse and lawn lead down
toward beauty. William Redfield
speeds his steamboat
up to Hartford...

It is the Twentieth Century—
Irish, Swedes, and Italians
cross the river to the quarries,
splitting brownstone
to raise families.
Brutal work for little pay.

It is 1938—you see the Arrigoni,
largest bridge in New England,
symbol of our strength and pride
yet with grace in its design,
stunning feat of engineering,
bold endeavor of its time.
For more than fifty of its years
it glowed in bright industrial green
like the emerald aquamarine
of beryl buried near it.

It is now the Twenty-first Century—
the bridge is a mostly modern shade
of dull municipal blue.
But there are times in early mornings

when the water's surface flattens
as the mists rise into ghost clouds
and the river turns to sky forever
and the bridge
in mirrored symmetry
becomes a pair of haunting eyes
bemused and bespectacled,
demanding of the boats a toll.
The ancient spirit hovers, glares,
dares intrepid travelers
to pass through.

Choose any bank
on any lazy afternoon
down by the river sideways
lying with your ear to the ground,
you'll be lulled into its current,
immense motion
running through you,
and you'll contemplate its bend
and the wending ways of folks
who came here in unending
streams of lives enroute to there,

and tomorrow you will leave here,
say goodbye and pack off to
north south east west
New York Moscow Baghdad Rome—
you'll return to chosen rivers,
knowing rivers take you back.

To Middletown

April 18, 2006

I've loved you like a good citizen should:
a place where rivers and canoes converge,
in spring a blooming blushing,
in fall a wind-tossed day.
I've loved you in drunken revelry in
Barnum's, La Boca, Gatekeepers,
the Brass Rail, the March In Tavern...
I've slept with your legends
under your stars on Indian Hill:
Major General Joseph King Fenno Mansfield,
Jesse Baldwin, George Washington,
Dr. Joseph Barratt and Dr. Kate Hurd Mead.
I've jogged and sinned
in your church market streets.
I have roots here, I have family.
Politicians have maligned me here
on several occasions, and
I've felt hatred here, like a fire closing in.
And yet, Middletown, you always
give me reason to proceed with grace
on some no-count O'Rourke's Diner afternoon.

Nocturne

And this town is so happening some nights
it makes me go wandering
just to hear the music of people laughing
and I follow the star trail and I listen, listen.

The Day the Poets Came to Middletown

Phrases in bold were taken from poems heard at the 1997 International Poetry Slam in Middletown, CT.

Sleepy old Middletown, barely awake
almost wasn't ready for the souls
who made streets shake
like giants were walking down her sidewalks,
like healers pulling out miracles
for every just-off-welfare, tired-of-fightin'
or politi-tangled or academic-strangled
or just plain media-mangled refugee
hanging out on Main Street.
And the usually oppressive
river-valley-one-hundred-degree
August-in-Middletown air
instead came rolling down
through our blocks from ancient skies
clean and cool-fresh, brilliant-breathed
because the streets were quaking,
and made the wind play like dolphins
in the rejuvenating blue.
The Muses conspired and made that cool—
they bestowed that cool on Middletown
for the poets' invasion. They made us all
turn off our freaking noisy air
conditioners in our separate
numbered houses. Made us open

our windows to hear the song
on the wind. Made us get out
and meet faces on the street.
Years ago this sad lady knew
how to dance, knew how to stroll
down sycamore lanes to the river,
knew where the rock was. But
her children started fighting
over who gets this and who gets that
of her splendid love til one day she up and jumped
off the bridge her own bounty had inspired
and drowned herself in the river.
It took an army of poets, the roving
collected un-dead of spiritual clarity
to raise her back up. And did she dance?
Did she! She'd been waiting for the chance.
Pulse, slowly, barely *bum bum*
soul strut *bum bum*
sensual flowers in her young body *bum bum*
Coltrane evocation *Bum Ba,* **rarefied in**
Arkansas *Bum Ba*
slave to the rhythm *Bum Ba*
Everyone is checking "Other" *Bum Ba*
A'int I African? *Bum ba* **Ameri can I fit in?** *Bum ba*
Amerika ka ka? *Ka BUM*
ghetto beauty *Ka BUM* **national sins** *Ka BUM*
not available in Cuba *Ka BUM Ba Ka BUM Ba*
Ka BUM Ba Ka BUM Ba
The poets fall asleep at dawn, dreaming
rhapsodically, well-sourced and deep...

The revival is over. They'll pack their bags,
quietly retreat, migrate like random gypsies,
back to families, homes, "real" jobs,
back to dealing with the pain and the changes
of worlds that need them. The unions of dreamers,
shamans, healers, voices, tongues
disperse…

And the un-sad lady stretches her limbs
and she realizes she is still alive. She
shakes off her gritty blooms in thanks
for a poet to catch a glimpse of out a car window
heading west, east, north, south...
The sky, river, wind dance in her.
Her children are beaming
Ka BUM Ba Ka BUM Ba Ka BUM Ba Ka BUM Ba

Rapallo Avenue

Howdy neighbor, what do you say?
It's going to be a happy day.
Greet your neighbor and boogie on down,
Give him a bump and turn around.

Children's song heard on Rapallo Avenue,
Middletown, Connecticut, 1989

You hear lots of people on the street
in conversation, when friends meet:
Hey, yo, porque? Si, bien, eh?
Sup? chillin chillin, word, no way...

You think you understand it all, like Jazz.
You feel it but don't know it has
roots buried deep under these sidewalks.
You just like the way she talks.

Into spirit, stories are told
and into music sung like old
nursery rhymes in parking lots
empty but for children's thoughts

of dinner, skip rope, *Mommy's man*
Hit in his head with a frying pan,
How many stitches did he get?
Uno dos tres quatro cinqo ses

siete... ocho... neuve...
dies... Dinner aroma alleyway
lullaby lasagna catfish fried
chicken fresh bread sausage pork pie,

fried rice curried spice yams pizza
Jamaican patties from Ortiz
Scaciatta calzone pastry
at Santa Maria Bakery.

And up in apartments and down the halls,
there's music, families, languages, all
the food's on the table—recipes honed—
with flavors that taste just like home.

And in the breeze the flavors meet
the free air rhythms of the street
where words from windows fall into
open ears on Rapallo Avenue.

Normal Day

It is a normal day near Thanksgiving,
the sky a child's brush stroke, cerulean
watercolor across the whole North End,
ending at the insurance ziggurat.
Delivery trucks stock Mom and Pop shops
along Main Street—Public Market, Ortiz's,
Vinci's, First Wok, It's Only Natural...
Frank is at his fish truck talking nonstop.
Local morning news faces the sidewalks
with black, white and Kool-Aid-colored print
in wire racks made further down the street.
A few chalkboards announce the day's specials.
Meanwhile, Kim Quinones the activist
unloads found bicycle parts into an
old abandoned storefront. Her dream is to
fix them all—each stolen or abandoned
wheel attached to every broken body,
renewed, sanded, painted the corn-yellow
color of taxicabs and school buses
so everyone in town can get around.
A Salvation Army truck pulls onto
Main Street, bed full of Salvation Santas
including Mr. Gypsy Zecharesh
heading off to ring their bells on corners.
They pass Henry, who is putting fliers
on kiosks. He thinks we should all build a
place for kids who, understandably, find

Main Street much more interesting than school.
The merchants dress their shops for the season.
I pass a drunk man standing beneath two
angels taped to a store window. He asks
me out for a drink, still smiling as I
decline. A young couple walk arm in arm,
reminding us all of sensual warmth.
Old wobbly Stanley yells a hoarse “Hello!”
his red cap pointing to an all blue sky.

Initial Conditions

Upon Indian Hill
and down to the river
the grape leaves
follow the moving current.
I've seen pigeons, crows,
turkey buzzards from the dump,
occasionally a seagull
and once a peregrine—
all in my backyard.
Outside I hear
the commotion of Squirrel
about the compost.
My neighbor thinks my yard's a mess—
out her window
wild and uncivilized
snake and weed and possum.

Local Color

The neighborhood is full tonight.
We walk, hang out,
talk to strangers about
why they call that building the Arriwani
or watch that same strange man dance
when they play music in the garden.
“How in tune he is,” you say, “how beautifully
he dances.” Some of the tourists call him drunk,
but not you—
you see things differently.
You see old bottles lying around
in the gold, dried grass
like hobos, full of emptiness
and shining in the sun.
Sometimes you climb mountains
deep in thought
and you don’t even notice
until you see valleys stretch out before you
and it takes your breath away—
the valleys are deep and green,
like an enormous ocean
frozen into steep crested waves
and you are suspended above it,
instantly timeless.
You recall the last time it happened—
when you met Marylin on Main Street,
who talks in thirty-foot long-jumps.

You found yourself stranded between her thoughts,
staring at the great valley
while she went ahead, hopscotch down Main Street—
woman who makes the hills and the mountains
by leaping with the moon,
muttering nonsense with her lips.
And when she shows up late for the music
the two of you greet like the sidewalk
legends you are, lost luminaries
who've survived imagination's demise.

Hartford Sidewalk Child

There is a child of forgetting
chasing the rocks he has thrown
on a sidewalk in Hartford.
He says to me: “Do you think
I can throw this rock
higher than the sky?”
“No way,” I say. He takes the dare,
he throws it up high
and it disappears completely.
We look at each other, speechless.
We have just witnessed a miracle
together. He walks off humming
a tune, which I recognize—
No woman no cry.
Angels follow him.
I feel them come to me.

Sister on the Sidewalk

Hello, I am your sister.
What is that you say?
Am I a spy?
Well, of course I am—
I am a spy in the house of fear,
I am making sure the coast is clear,
safe enough for soul
to step out on the town,
find some place to be.
Hello, I am your sister.
Pardon if I seem rude
but I've been among the loveless
for so long
I have soul longing.
The body gets weary
bones want to crash
skin seeks waves of warm blood
body craves nourishment
and mind craves attention.
If you don't understand this
then you are just in my way.
If you have the time, then let's talk.

Wearing my Walkman Downtown

I hear the music of Japanese koto
as I come upon
a landlord yelling.
A young mother
is wasting water by filling
a small pool for her son.
The son looks up bewildered at
the landlord, who is red,
gesticulating angrily.
I can see electric needles
scatter from his mouth, his
fist. He must be screaming.
But mostly I hear
this beautiful music.
The son looks at me.
I pray that someday
they may all hear
and be soothed by
this strange music,
composed it seems
by someone more familiar with water.

Out this Window: Patient Record

The same beauty and pain as anywhere.
The golden Maxfield Parrish light
on the building across the street
and the way the pigeons reflect
the sun and send their shadows
in brief array as they circle and return.
There is always beauty. There is always pain.
There is an emaciated prostitute
who sits on the geraniums
in the window box. She is not here now.
I can see the broken stems.
She is dying, will not speak to us.
From this window I see people
who have no money in the richest state
in the richest country in the world,
no homes, no futures, no jobs:
addicted to crack, alcohol,
abuse. Some are dying
and they either know it or don't.
There is the girl with the colostomy bag
selling herself for a hit. There are the old men
waiting for the next high.
These are not the hollow men—
they say hello every day, they are kind,
they have howled in the wasteland.
They are not evil, just incurably lost. Meanwhile,
the scavengers of the new wasteland are many—

the creeps and the politicians and the buyers
and the sellers and owners and even some of
the social workers in their brand new jobs.
And all the suits walk by so quickly, can't say hello
because they are card-carrying members of
the time-is-money cult or the efficiency cult
or the just plain nasty folks cult.
Two men on the corner, both dying, ragged, slow,
smile at each other and join in warm embrace.

War No More

Gonna lay down my sword and shield
Down by the riverside
Ain't gonna study war no more.

Traditional gospel song

How to Get Food on the Table in a Small Post-industrial City

Josie lives upstairs above Master Supply.
The doors are always locked and there
are no buzzers. To visit you must yell
to the windows upstairs for
someone to come downstairs to let you in.
But you can't yell from Main Street
because the police substation is there
and they always come out and yell at you
so you have to walk all the way around to the back
and scream louder than six car radios.

Yesterday, Josie, who has lived in that building
longer than God, who has fed, housed,
and clothed half the people who
have passed through, Josie, whom
everyone knows, to whom everyone goes
to get coffee, sanity, or chicken, after going through
the local assistance agency bureaucracies—
Josie, who should be clad in jewels
to match her gospel voice,
just wanted to get her groceries upstairs.

A friend drove her to the grocery store, and when
they got back they honked the horn
to get her grandkids down
to carry the groceries up.

Well, two folks get out of their car
the same time she does and they yell, “Don’t honk!”
Like she’s no one. “Don’t you know people are sleeping!”
Well, now since Josie’s been there for years taking
care of everyone white, black, young and old
and never said nothing about anyone,

and since these white folks just moved in,
are not sleeping themselves,
and don’t say it like “Could you please not yell
because we are trying to sleep,” and
since these folks are just in her face yelling “Don’t!”
like they own the place,
well, they make Josie mad.
She tries to go at them but her friend
accompanies her upstairs
as others begin to yell
and cuss and when the cops finally barge in

she sets those scrawny cops straight.
People in her face, the whole building
yelling, kids running up to watch,
cops banging on the door,
when—after working all day
and looking for a new apartment
but being turned down on the phone
because of the sound of her voice—
Josie, who holds together most of the neighborhood,
just wanted to get her groceries upstairs.

Western Civilization

So it's out of the blue
and into the world
and it's dealing
but with only a busted raft
half-masted, ass backward,
lacking unity,
greedy for dry land.

And then there come
gas-guzzling "cigarette boats"
out of control, 120 mph,
calling themselves "sea angels,"
spewing flotsam in their wake
and setting the oceans on fire,

not to mention
the love boat battleship circus cruises,
the blue water sum of our history.
No wonder soul hides,
won't meet me at the port,
cries *Abort! Abort!*

The Cow Is For Us

The cow is for us for us,
the cow is for us for us,
sacrificial worker mother
for us, for us!

The cow is for us for us,
the cow is for us for us,
milk and blood and meat
for us, for us!

The cow is for us for us,
the cow is for us for us,
manure for our farms
for us for us!

The cow is for us for us,
the cow is for us for us,
leather for our feet
for us for us!

The cow is for us for us,
the cow is for us for us,
and we shall consume
for us for us!

The cow is for us for us,
the cow is for us for us
all over this bloody earth
for us. For us!

bushland

March 23, 2003 – 10:40 p.m.

There is lightning and thunder
in Middletown. From my window
it looks and sounds like air strikes
to the west. While the more belligerent of us
unite in war, the rest of us huddle, in fear.

In bushland we watch well-groomed
reporters accompanied by
digital graphic displays of how the
bunker-busters hit their targets
with precision.

“Nyaa nyaa nyaa nyaa nyaa
I’m getting my dad and he has a gun.”

Tonight through this lightning
and this thunder, and the bombs,
and the bloodshed, as the cradle
of civilization is obliterated,
may God/Allah bless this world.

Skirting Disaster

Wake up sisters, hos,
mothers and other irrational women
to our wildest sides.
We are needed at this time.
There are things they just don't see,
though our brothers
are not evil, they are
blind to moons and tides.
The ancient shamanic
Karma-Mama is dancing again,
whirling dervishly,
lifting all her skirts.
Stirring and gathering
unscrupulous winds
violently streaking the sky
electric dark.

She stomps
on the ground of the dead
whom she bore.
She can't stand this
goddess-damned war.

She dances a dance for
pasty politicians
corporate jungle heroes
right wing Christians

power-crazed narcissists
mealy-mouthed marauders
spoiled rich oilers
slliced and fresh shoppers
nasty closet creepos
rocket-eyed scientists
fortune-eyed maniacs.
She will dance for anyone
whose moral authority
separates him
from herself.

A Short Poem
for the Month of May

We who believe
we are so right—
well-referenced, strong,
properly titled and attired
for tragically victorious wars—
are occasionally
fortunate enough
to fail and fall,
through grace, contrite.

About the Author

Susan Allison lives in Middletown, Connecticut with her husband, Stephan, and son, John. Born in Derby, Connecticut and raised in Louisville, Kentucky, she calls poetry and wanderlust the two main constants in her life. After mountain-climbing and hitch-hiking through East Africa, she returned to Wesleyan University to earn a BA in African Studies in 1985. Shortly after graduation, she discovered used and rare bookstores, which became new destination points for her wanderlust until she opened her own, Ibis Books & Gallery, in 1989. The bookstore was transformed in 1991 into NEAR, Inc./The Buttonwood Tree, an arts and cultural performance space on Main Street in Middletown, Connecticut.

Down by the Riverside Ways is set in Helvetica. The development and exponential growth of this font was a product of Modernism. Created by Max Miedinger with Eduard Hoffmann in 1957 for the Haas Type Foundry in Münchenstein, Switzerland, Helvetica displays a clarity and simplicity that has rejuvenated attitudes to and uses of design. Though it was originally called Neue Hass Grotesk, in 1960 the font was renamed Helvetica, the Latin name for Switzerland.

◊

To order additional copies of this book
or other Antrim House titles, contact the publisher at

Antrim House
P.O. Box 111, Tariffville, CT 06081
860.217.0023, AntrimHouse@comcast.net
or the house website (www.AntrimHouseBooks.com).

•

On the house website
are sample poems, upcoming events,
and a "seminar room" featuring discussion topics
& writing suggestions offered by Antrim House authors
as well as supplemental biography, notes, images and poems.